"I Never Promised You an Apple Orchard" The Collected Writings of SNOOPY

"I Never Promised You an Apple Orchard" The Collected Writings of SNOOPY

Being a compendium of his puns, correspondence, cautionary tales, witticisms, titles original and borrowed, with critical commentary by his friends, and, published for the first time in its entirety, the novel *"Toodle-oo, Caribou!" A Tale of the Frozen North*

CHARLES M. SCHULZ

Holt, Rinehart and Winston
New York

Library of Congress Catalog Card Number: 75-21464

ISBN: 0-03-017216-0

Printed in the United States of America

10 9 8 7 6 5 4 3 2 1

For Joanne Greenberg, of course

Edith had refused to marry him
because he was too fat.

"Why don't you go on a diet?" suggested
a friend. "You can't have your cake and
Edith, too!"

Though her husband often went on business trips, she hated to be left alone.

"I've solved our problem," he said. "I've bought you a Saint Bernard. Its name is Great Reluctance. Now when I go away, you shall know that I am leaving you with Great Reluctance!"

She hit him with a waffle iron.

HEE
HEE
HEE
HEE

His wife had always hated his work. "You'll never make any money growing toadstools," she complained.

"On the contrary," he declared. "My toadstool business is mushrooming!"

She creamed him with the electric toaster.

Joe Anthro was an authority on Egyptian and Babylonian cultures. His greatest accomplishment, however, was his famous work on the Throat Culture.

A few thoughts concerning a lost love . . .

Rats!

"You've always ignored me," she said. "And now you say you want to marry me. Every night you play cards. I'm really afraid that you love cards more than you love me. If you could say something nice to me just once, perhaps I'd marry you."

"  "

"You blew it!" she said, and walked out of his life forever.

"Dear Contributor,
   Thank you for submitting your manuscript. We regret that it does not suit our present needs."

Her real name was Dorothy Fledermaus, but all her friends called her "Dee." Thus, she was frequently referred to as "Dee Fledermaus."

The last car drove away. It began to rain. And so our hero's life ended as it had begun . . . a disaster. "I never got any breaks," he always complained.

He had wanted to be rich. He died poor. He wanted friends. He died friendless. He wanted to be loved. He died unloved. He wanted laughter. He found only tears.

He wanted applause. He received boos.
He wanted fame. He found only obscurity.
He wanted answers. He found only
questions.

They had named their Great Dane
"Good Authority."

One day, she asked her husband if he
had seen her belt.

"Belt?" he said. "Oh, I'm sorry. I thought
it was a dog collar. I have it on Good
Authority."

Shortly thereafter, their marriage
began to go downhill.

Immediately after he won the golf tournament, he was interviewed on TV.

"This is the most exciting moment of my life!" he said.

"I saw you on TV," said his wife. "I thought the day we got married was the most exciting moment of your life."

In the next tournament, he failed to make the cut.

"I love you," she said, and together they laughed. Then one day she said, "I hate you," and they cried. But not together.

The first time he saw her she was playing tennis.

"Ours was a Love Set," he said, "but we double-faulted."

THAT'S VERY GOOD..NOW ALL YOU NEED IS A TITLE...

A Love Story
by
Erich Beagle

"Do you love me?" she asked.

"Of course," he said.

"Do you really love me?" she asked.

"Of course," he said.

"Do you really really love me?"
she asked.

"No," he said.

"Do you love me?" she asked.

"Of course," he said.

So she asked no more.

"Our love will last forever," he said.
"Oh, yes! yes! yes!" she cried.
"Forever being a relative term, however," he said.
She hit him with a ski pole.

"Dear Contributor,
    We think your new story is magnificent.
We want to print it in our next issue, and
will pay One Thousand Dollars."

"P.S. April Fool!"

This is a tale of Greed.

Joe Greed was born in a small town in Colorado.

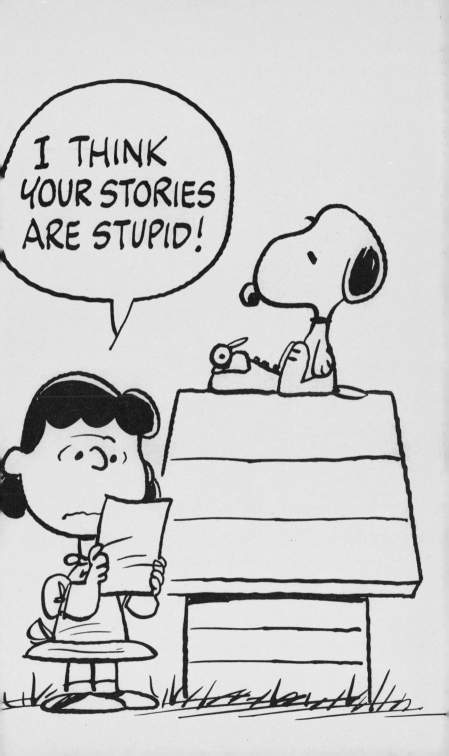

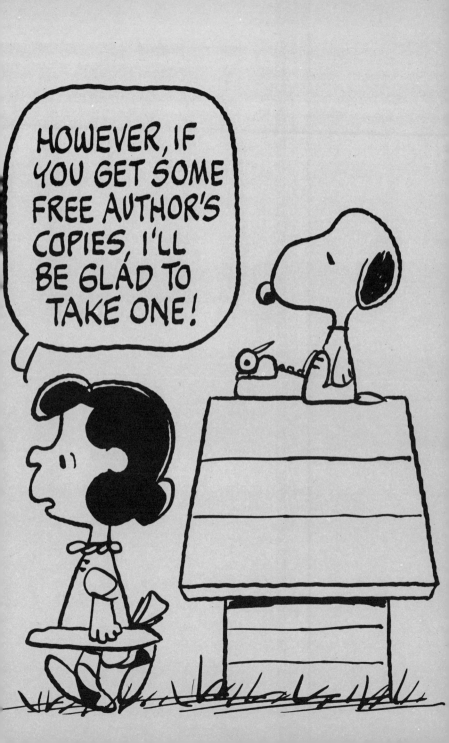

To Whom It May Concern

Dear Whom:

The Bunnies . . . A Tale of Mirth and Woe
"Ha Ha Ha," laughed the bunnies.
"Ha Ha Ha Ha Ha Ha Ha Ha Ha Ha"

Joe Sportscar spent ten thousand dollars on a new twelve-cylinder Eloquent.

"You think more of that car than you do of me," complained his wife. "All you ever do these days is wax Eloquent!"

This is the story of two mice who lived in a museum.

One evening after the museum had closed, the first mouse crawled into a huge suit of armor. Before he knew it, he was lost. "Help!" he shouted to his friend. "Help me make it through the knight!"

"Dear Contributor,
 Thank you for submitting your story to our magazine. To save time, we are enclosing two rejection slips..."

"One for this story, and one for the next story you send us."

Bug Off!!

A Tale of Two Cities

Of Human Bondage

"Toodle-oo, Caribou!"
A Tale of the Frozen North

Other books by the author

It Was a Dark and Stormy Night

One morning Joe Eskimo went out to his barn to milk his polar cow. As he walked through the barn, tiny polar mice scampered across the frozen floor.

The stall was empty!

"Someone has stolen my polar cow!" shouted Joe Eskimo. "This is the work of Joe Jacket, who hates me!"

Joe Eskimo and Joe Jacket were rivals for the heart of Sally Snow who lived south of the iceberg. Joe Eskimo thought back to the night when he first shook her hand. Now, he was about to lose her.

Quickly, he harnessed his dog team and sped into town. He found Joe Jacket and Sally Snow sitting in a small café drinking polar tea.

"You'll never take Sally Snow away from me, you scoundrel!" shouted Joe Eskimo.

"And just what do you think you're going to do about it?" sneered Joe Jacket.

"Stop it, you two!" said Sally Snow. "You're creating a scene. I don't want to marry either of you. I've decided to join the Women's Tennis Tour. That's where the money is!"

"You don't know how to play tennis," said Joe Eskimo.

"I can learn, can't I? There's a pro out at the club who's giving group lessons. I'm going to sign up."

"Do you have a racket?" asked Joe Jacket.

"Of course," said Sally. "I bought one today."

"Wood or metal?"

"Wood, of course. I'm a traditionalist."

"Gut or nylon?"

"Gut, if you must know! And now, if you'll excuse me, I'm going to take my first lesson. Thank you for the polar tea. Toodle-oo, Caribou!"

Thus, Joe Eskimo and Joe Jacket became good friends, having been driven together by the same shattering blow. They worked the polar ranch together, and eventually became very wealthy.

Sally Snow went on to become only a mediocre player, for her volley was weak. After three years on the tour, she married an Australian who struck her from behind one day during a mixed-doubles match.

"When will you learn to stay on your side of the court?" he shouted.

Sally began to cry, and ran off to the locker room. That evening she took a plane to Vancouver. From her hotel room she placed a phone call to Joe Eskimo in Alaska.

"Hello, Joe? Is that you, Joe?" she sobbed.

"Which Joe do you want?"

"Which Joe?"

"Yes, there are two Joes living here. Which Joe do you wish to speak to?"

"Oh, forget it!" said Sally, and she hung up.

The snow began to fall gently past the window of her hotel room, and the lights of the city sparkled below. Sally lay back on the bed, sighed, and closed her eyes. "Toodle-oo, Caribou!" she said.

Gentlemen,

I have just completed my new novel. It is so good, I am not even going to send it to you.

Why don't you just come and get it?

Gentlemen,
   Yesterday, I waited all day for you to come and get my novel and to publish it, and make me rich and famous. You did not show up. Were you not feeling well?

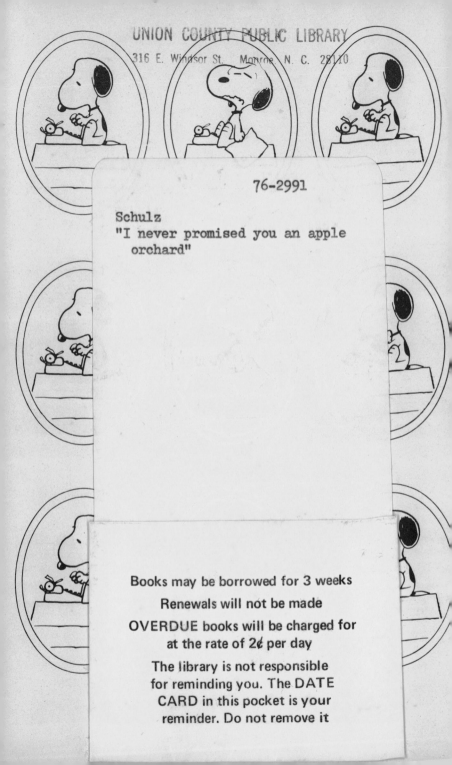